T0304329

DURATIONS

TED PEARSON

DURATIONS

selva oscura press • chicago, illinois

"Return to Silence" #4 first appeared in *Creative Flight* (India).

Published by selva oscura press
selvaoscurapress.com

First Edition
ISBN 978-0-9909453-8-3

Design and typesetting by Margaret Tedesco
Text set in Le Havre and ITC Galliard
Printing: McNaughton & Gunn

Cover image, *littoral* by Ken Taylor ©2010

Distributed by Small Press Distribution
1341 Seventh Street, Berkeley, CA 94710
www.spdbooks.org

a 501(c)(3) nonprofit

for Clark & Susan Coolidge

FOREWORD

Ted Pearson's new volume of poems, *Durations*, is paralyzingly simple only until Pearson springs upon the reader what the poems are about, and what they are about doing. The poems seem to be about writing poetry, but really, they are about the fever, the fervor that breaks the paralysis, the seizure, the complacent holing up that has stricken these times of pandemic, political catastrophe, and racial reckoning. These poems, in their reclaiming bewilderedness, possibly start the new conscience on a path from paralyzed stasis toward healing.

No specific characters are named other than in mythological or literary allusion. This is also the case with specifics of place, so the poem seems to be lacking any particular location or period. The time of the poems is also debatable: "the day after the author died." The book is dedicated to Clark and Susan Coolidge, and each of the three serial poems opens with a quoted epigraph. "Zeno Effect," with a quote from Morton Feldman, "Screenshots," with one from Richard Diebenkorn, and "Return to Silence," with one from Miguel de Unamuno. Which author is actually referenced? Or is it the poet as a trope musing mortality?

With no apparent thematic focus, the poems might appear to be about abstraction, but Pearson has this line in the "Return to Silence" #13:

> Hard truths occupy local space-time

from which current readers may recall the Occupy Movement of late local Wall Street time and place. So, the specifics are actually present in the structural arrangements of the allusions, images, idioms used in the construction of the poems.

Pearson has a peculiar way with meme, cliché, idiom. The words themselves have almost no meaning anymore, but the poet knows that they retain even after that loss, a certain feeling, an argument of affect. When he lays out the specific landscape of disasters, and the actions staged across it that have brought the culture to this seizure, this holing up in lies, he often realizes that a reasoned layout of the facts will be incomprehensible. So, against that enemy, he offers an empathy, a familiar common poetry: the sayings and clichés that we all know, but also know that they don't mean what they say or seem to. Pearson throws to the reader the affective argument, a feeling, which is what we know we want. Another way to say this is, Pearson offers the reader her own critique. He has given to her, her own familiar dismantled in her own explanation, and it suddenly rings false. She has to create in order to reinstate meaning. So, the poems *are* about writing.

Pearson writes a lyric for what he's doing, a lyric of what is in operation here. In "Return to Silence" #13, he also writes:

> Once we're working, our practice reveals, what affect
> teaches, we think to feel.

That is the printed lineation, but camouflaged within those lines are these lines:

> Once we're working
> our practice reveals
> what affect teaches
> we think to feel.

This version is a quatrain reminiscent of Pearson's persistent earlier verse rigor:

1st line	4 syllables	feminine ending	
2nd line	5 syllables	masculine ending	rhymed
3rd line	5 syllables	feminine ending	
4th line	4 syllables	masculine ending	rhymed

Also, notice the sonic patterning of these lines:

1st line	2 (+ 1 implied) "W" sounds.
2nd line	opens with extension of closing sound of line 1 ("work" / "our") echoing opening vowel sounds "once" and "our."
3rd line	opens with "what," and the "a" sound in "affect" echoes "practice" in the 2nd line.
4th line	opens with "we"; "feel" rhymes with "reveal" in its 2nd line, but more precisely, "reveal" rhymes exactly with "we". . ."feel."

Verse pattern bears out argument here almost in a graphic of illustration.

affect = practice
reveal = we feel

The reader hardly has to think it through; she can 'see' these equations.

The printed version and the implicit version never meet, though they act upon each other and seem to be an example of Zeno's image of parallels, a depiction of the relation between language per se and language about. They exist together: one in a didactic, graphically familiar free verse, the other implied by the echoic music of a familiar historical form.

Pearson writes:

where writing intersects the discourse on writing,
there's little back and forth

The two never meet. There's writing and then there's discourse *about* writing. There seems to be no hope of mutual understanding. Yet, Pearson disrupts the prosaic by embedding the camouflaged lineation of metrical writing, a recognition of the *sound* of the tradition of rhymed metrical verse. Intruding between the two is his way of simultaneously disrupting and promoting further understanding. He does not deny Zeno's understanding, but he also does not admit to hopelessness. His response, while not the old redemptive hope, is a freedom from easy false hope. If there is any response worth having, he seems to be saying, it is a responsible movement of re-creation by working creatively toward a restored world, a participation in its duration.

Pearson may have camouflaged his rectitudinous style, but the vigor of his thinking continues openly throughout the pages of his book.

—Ed Roberson

THE ZENO EFFECT

It appears to me that the subject of music
. . . has always been its construction.

— Morton Feldman

1.

Universals are hard to come by,

        which explains our recourse to

                opacity. I remember the day

the author died, the second Friday

        in September. I have no doubt that

                all he wanted was for his work

to endure. Who broke with

        convention, embraced invention,

                and with it the empire of signs.

Meanwhile, echoes edified the head-

        lands with Pentecostal rhythms

                and roisterous rimes. Such is

the allure of poetic license. Few can

        resist the Sirens' song, but none

                can survive their silence.

2.

We woke to find our horizon in

     flames. While the future burned

          bright with palpable illusions,

the present collapsed amid fading

     embers. Hooded eyes battened on

          nubile youth, for whom ex-

patriation was the height of privilege.

     Whose parody of exile passed for

          a style. Then the conundrum

that precedes last call: when

     and with whom will you go

          home? And how is that better

than being alone? You'll know

     when your key doesn't fit the lock.

          There *is* no private paradiso.

3.

We had grave doubts we could

      find safe haven — after the deluge,

            before the rapture, and without

commercial interruption. We

      sought revelation, not annotation.

            Unstable meanings made for

strained relations. Then came

      the moment of epochal change

            with the passage from work

to text. That was the moment

      the reader was born and the

            author abandoned the game.

Whose loss was a blow

      to the order of things

            for want of a proper name.

4.

Listen hard: it's all in the silences.

    Even as, amid the embers, dis-

        cordant songs of earth and air

stirred and stoked and stanched at will

    an intermittent blaze. One which

        brings us light and heat and

the aromatic smoke of hellfire.

    Still, you chose to ride it out and

        hoped to see tomorrow. While

I found every good reason to flee

    from memories made in sorrow.

    And so it was I hit the

road and sang the miles away. There

    will be no rest till the Grail appears

        on the cusp of Judgment Day.

5.

Better to have mourned the day

       you were born than wait till the

              bitter end. That's when there's

nothing more to be done.

       That's when your failures

              and incapacities have overrun

your dreams. Better to have grieved

       while there was reason to hope

              for a better outcome, an end

to your pain. Reason enough to

       forgo these rites and avoid

              standing here in the rain.

Where a hillside grave overlooks

       the bay, whose waters gave

              life and then took it away.

6.

Scenes of insatiable youth

        are trifles. It's a bitter wind

                that bends us to its will.

Still, we salute their

        memory, which now burns

                low, yet lingers still.

It's hard to imagine further

        austerities when life is

                already rife with precarity.

We've labored for years

        our fate to construe.

                The end, when it comes,

will tell us true. The one

        who says "I" is the one

                who loves "you."

7.

All we know of our fathers is

        conjecture. Lyrics were added

                the following year. Whence,

"the surplus production of power"

        remains among our abiding fears.

                Ours was a village of widows

and orphans. After the war came

        famine and plague. Thus, were our

                hopes for the future dashed,

leaving us only dust and ash.

        Where we had hoped to be

                set free, our leaders sought to

avoid the lash. Staying the whip-

        hand fulfilled a promise. Now,

                fresh chains lie heavy upon us.

8.

When is a crux not also a crucible?

      When will we at last see through the

            present appearance of things?

Given time, your illusions falter. Even

      as your ambition wanes. At dusk,

            you vanish into the tain.

"Depart to love and new noises."

      Music to make these old heads spin.

            Outside language, storm winds

howl. But, though you hoped to

      escape the din, yours is a tale

            of evolving sorrow. The night-

shift chills to bluesy sounds. Then,

      it's time to complete your rounds

            and start again tomorrow.

9.

The bodies are starting to fall too

       fast, even to eulogize the lot

              of them. Haunted eyes reflect

the fear that attends we know not

       what. Whence, the unthinkable

              becomes invisible, a condition

of the moment to which none are

       immune. Who among you expected

              to win this war we've made

on nature? Extinction events

       are ever more common.

              Avoiding them is wise.

Albeit the universe couldn't

       care less, karma dictates

              our certain demise.

10.

Which half of the glass is empty? What

        might this ill wind beget? In a trope that's

                harder to forgive than forget,

the Magus imagined that alchemy

        preceded political economy, which

                might explain his poverty,

if not his nostalgia for shtick.

        Things are famously what they

                are in a world that is what it is.

Where public discourse spawns

        such phrases, we watch the news

                with dumbstruck faces.

Cynics praise our honesty as

        one step up from mockery,

                our once and future home.

11.

And so we come to our least

       likely subject, doubly enmeshed in

              a world of strife. What begins

in fantasy eventuates as fact.

       What steered his sleep now rules

              his waking life. Signs and

wonders fuel his dread. Breath

       distinguishes the living from

              the dead. In certain genres,

the common touch affirms what

       is commonly said. Something

              about a woman and a song.

And something audiences

       seem to love about someone

              doing somebody wrong.

12.

Midway along life's journey, it was

    finally time for drinks. We'd

        been hiking all day on

Dharma Mountain — the kind of

    mountain that comes and goes,

        depending on your state

of mind. Ensconced in a tavern

    in the shadow of the summit,

        we drank to our abjection.

At issue were the optics of our

    recent depression, an issue that calls for

        great circumspection. In time,

our grievances may get an airing.

    But first we must reconcile art and

        life. A most inapposite pairing.

13.

The video began with a brief montage.

Borderlands made up the mise en

scène. The soundtrack featured

Sonic Toxin, she of the poisonous

pen. Whose sex life stunned her

loyal fans was part panther,

part hierophant. There were un-

stated reasons behind her decline.

And unreasoned statements,

far from kind. Will there be no end to

interpretation? To half-truths

hoping to be made whole?

Or to half-lives looking to come in

from the cold? The sun

grows weaker as we grow old.

14.

Who wears the withered laurels

        of defeat knows whereof he

                speaks. Knows of needs that

exceed propriety and the Void of

        form that seeks satiety. Knows

                full well his time is brief.

Granted, it's hard to be heard

        over thunder. Granted, it's

                tempting to sleep all day. Still,

he insists on having his say.

        Firmly resolved to ride out

                the storm, he cautions us,

if we stay the course, there

        are no words to shelter us

                and keep us safe from harm.

15.

What exactly was "holy and

        wond'rous" that wasn't a danger

                to itself? Uncanny doubles

pledged their allegiance. Twins

        were entwined with their better

                halves. These were omens

which made it clear that

        none would survive the flood.

                Our texts, like the poor, are

always with us. And, like

        the wealthy, of little use.

                Negativity is our life's blood.

To reprise, what we sought was

        "holy and wond'rous," but not

                without danger to ourselves.

16.

A score is not its realization.

      You try living in a blueprint.

           During the war, we huddled

in cisterns. After the deluge,

      we were swept away. In broad

           outline, there's a powerful bond

between the forces that brought

      us together and those that

           drove us apart. "In order

to form a more perfect union,"

      form must be more than an

           empty vessel. Even without a

score to guide us, the language

      game remains in play. Who fear

           the outcome will rue the day.

17.

How reconcile the spirit

      world with the physical facts of

            your existence? Note the forms

life takes as it passes. Particles

      of light align like choristers,

            ready to chronicle the day's

defeats. Sound waves rock

      the vernacular cradle.

            Together, they are pleased to

confirm once more "that the play

      begins with the world." Escapist

            tales of Paradise offer no fit end

to dreaming. Only those touched

      by reality's spark will find

            their way home in the dark.

18.

A hard-pressed past confers a future where-

       in the enigma of invention balks at the

              very repetitions that we prize.

Let here and now follow where

       and when. There's ample reason

              to stay in character. To be

whomever you need to be. The maestro

       assures us that there is not

              and never was a present.

As if art and life were eponyms

       for that which shall remain nameless.

              For that which bridges past

and future. And dwells as lack

       in the House of Desire (as loss

              in the Realm of the Real).

19.

We've had it with these eulogies

      for times we never shared. Even

            as his memory fails, he spends

his days beyond the pale. He knew

      his time was running out. They were

            near the end of the set. He'd

hoped to hear just one more song.

      But he went without regret.

            The culture police had found

him out and he had to pay his debts.

      While one of many is second

            to none, none are without

some psychic scars. We've done the

      math and it doesn't add up. We

            are not what they say we are.

20.

Verfallen is the password for the Gates

　　　　of Hell. It was not an accident they

　　　　　　closed behind us. It was not by

chance we fell to Earth. Watch as

　　　　the master of educated guesses pivots

　　　　　　from paradigms to parables

of pain. Last night's program went

　　　　against the grain. The crowd was

　　　　　　unappeasable. Not long after,

a fecund Void appeared on the

　　　　plane of the feasible. And

　　　　　　from that Void all good things

beckon. Now, no matter

　　　　where we land, the inmates

　　　　　　think it's heaven.

21.

Sunlight poured through the roof

    of the world. Oracles bathed in

        the glow of prophecy. Artful

remnants of done deals betokened

    a past with shady conjugations.

        The provisional present

surrendered the city to the waiting

    embrace of its workers. After we

        plowed the suburbs under,

farms and vineyards thrived. Poets

    earned a living wage without

        ever having to leave the page

or give up words for things.

    The early autumn breeze that bites

        or the leaves of which we sing.

22.

I would be as a shadow on your

       wall, a mote of silence in

              the chaos that surrounds you,

a glint in the darkest corner of

       your eye. And, while no chord

              arrives unbroken, sonic shards

still constitute a music born to

       be written on the wind. Distance, not

              difference, has kept us apart.

Hope opines that we'll always

       have tomorrow. That's when

              we'll know what the future

has wrought. And that's where

       our legacies will flare or fade

              among the embers of thought.

23.

A booming bass fills the empty

      hours, a relentless pulse

            that rattles walls and secures

pride of place through repetition.

      The young can't escape the lure of

            the stage, where magical nights

follow insubstantial days.

      The old philosopher has left

            the capitol. Exile amounted to

silent soliloquies, followed by years

      of depression. We could

            only guess at the depths he

attained. This we attribute to his sense

      of discretion. And the years spent

            learning to welcome pain.

24.

Herewith, the supplement

       we bring to hiatus. The imaginary

              poet, in deep weeds, has fled

through a hole in the Real.

       Call it a refuge between

              catastrophes — *of* the world,

but not quite with it. Even

       as the elders railed against

              shortcuts, the maestro's sutures

made his name. Whence,

       we learned to parry and to

              bear our wounds with grace.

The resulting scars were lines of code

       that, taken together, made an ode

              and left behind this trace.

SCREENSHOTS

I can never accomplish what I want — only what I would have wanted had I thought of it beforehand.

— Richard Diebenkorn

1.

Weak sunlight at high noon filtered through the smoke of hellfire. It was a muggy day in late August. Tongues of flame leapt from broken windows. The old regime was coming apart. Even as they hoped to take us with them, we have thus far evaded death by attrition. Experience has taught us what little we know. It's hard to imagine the world at peace, a fact as painful as our own mortality. It's amazing how fragile these structures are. How so few could bring so many to ruin. What follows is based on doctrinal confusion. We say that in dreams begin recriminations. That thought resumes in the darkest hour. We balk at memories of early childhood, when how we lived before life happened was how we thought life was supposed to be.

2.

Only those who have seen the wind may invite the gong to sound. It's a matter of submission, not of will, when your task is to foreground the message. The perceptions that wake it, the affects that shape it, and the music of thought when we think. And, though its voicings may catch the ear, writing's "more formal than a field would be." Call it a dance between hand and eye. This reflects the history of writing and the evolution of type. I see the words that letters form as figures that begin with the hands that form them. And the form that follows is poetry. From prehistory's mysteries to the fleeting present, it gamely shelters those minims of data that spell our epochal discontent. Thus does it tarry, despite its travails, in the fecund womb of absurdity.

3.

Your story begins as the old world ends, leaving only you and a handful of friends. Much like the unsung singer and her song, empty promises have strung you along. But not to worry. Your day will come, trailing clouds and so forth. We hold these verses to be self-evident. That trauma short-circuits the grammar of thought. That songs are antidotes to what was lost when history went unheard. That too many act against their self-interest. That too few stand by their word. That every culture is an edifice of layers. Not least you yourself. That anarchy of the intellect leads to entropy of the will. That meaning issues from the empire of signs. And that your story, though rife with digressions, still leaves time to parse your lines.

4.

What were we thinking when the lights went out in the houses we once lived in? Not that there ever was a *we* but for two alone together. Friends observed a disaster in the making as affection foundered on the shoals of intimacy. By what analogy does love survive? What mode of thinking does loss engender? I suppose it's down to what one recalls — that lives were shared, and houses. Other memories follow suit, touching tableaux of romantic dinners and fervent late-night vows. But if vows were exchanged, I forget what was said. Proximity leads to enforced boundaries. That's when you know the spark is dead. The city, in principle, belongs to no one, yet these were the streets we walked along. And we thought of them as ours.

5.

Pictures efface the walls that absorb them. And that's precisely how custodial facts become curatorial nightmares. The challenges of transport made it difficult indeed to liberate these frescoes. Around which models draped themselves on the opening night of the show. Their faces were beacons of cosmetic art, de facto adverts for gilded cages. The rarest of birds, they never alight except for photo ops. Nor do they easily break a sweat. Much like those enfrescoed nymphs, they are fantasies which, albeit tempting, only mock reality. This leads to the questions you wanted to ask. The one where you wonder if goods and services are worth the wear and tear. And the one where you wonder whether without walls there would even *be* any pictures — or models to linger there.

6.

The writing on the wall said *without which, nothing*. In lieu of bedrock, we built on staves. And trusted our well-oiled timbers to shiver as the cabin walls echoed the ceaseless waves. She said, "There are times when I think of you often." Whose singular syntax fails to capture what time cannot forget. She herself, for one example. Chronic pain, for another. When all that's needed is a lucid account of sex with rhetorical devices. Whose lines trace the contours, unstable and oblique, of a homeland where the status quo is secretly unique. Where one wanted nothing more than to write, the other kept on writing. Zeno predicted the final result would be a map of motion. A map whose legend admonishes us that art is more than a notion.

7.

Before, there was nothing. Now, there's nothing much. What we
most distrust in others is what's missing in ourselves. I'm far less
certain I'll get this right than I am they'll get it wrong. And who
are they, but you, Dear Reader? The numbers say we are not alone.
You can check yourself in the mirror. And though I was never
fond of footnotes, in your case I'll make an exception. You have
studied the bitmap where our memories dwell. And you've sought
the improbable in all good things. You can still recall when peace
broke out, though it didn't last for long. But we give weight to the
evidence, even though it's thin. If it happened even once before,
peace could reign again. Such is our hope for those to come, but
who knows where or when?

8.

For the youngest among us these may seem to be missives from a
bygone world. A humdrum world less pressed by catastrophe, less
hemmed round by disaster. Or, what would be worse, a world that
viewed our most violent proclivities as normal. Which, be it said,
to our regret, they are. There's nothing short of the horizon to
arrest a gaze that carries beyond these walls. A gaze that longs for
the unhurried days that our faith in posterity promised. A steadfast
gaze that looks to the future from its perch in the dwindling present.
Where the breaking point between opposing forces is the point of
no return. Where there are no doors there are no locks, so we have
no use for keys. Nor for the myth of a bygone world where poets
took their ease.

9.

The Fates divided the Book of Outcomes into parts like Caesar's
Gaul. News of war receded in the weeks before the coup. The
Mistress of the Book had been terribly lonely. But our separate
season had come and gone. April in Paris explained everything. And
paved the way for a summer romance, which led to autumn in New
York. The poet, meanwhile, brought to light what long was hidden
from our view. Which made us wonder how he knew where to look.
And when he knew what he knew. Even as life is an open question,
it's a challenge living without answers in sight. The invisible world
has left no signs. Its counterpart yearns to be free. But the thought
police tell us to "Keep on moving. There's nothing here to see."

10.

In those years, life began after dark. First, we partied till break of
day. Then, we slept till the sun went away. At worst, the externals —
clouds and rain — were but the stuff of dreams. Our inner weather
called the tune. The world was our digression. But it wasn't simply
a case of extremes. There's a vast middle ground to be covered.
A world of towns where time's been reversed. Where dreams of
oblivion come and go, and life's more a matter of ebbs than flows.
The oracle brought out early footage of a future that doesn't include
you. Strands of meaning drifted past your once and future purview.
After siesta, "the sun sang the hours" and then it was twilight again.
And that's when you woke and became the one best known as you
to your friends.

11.

Not to presume upon the interest of others, but one did want to join the conversation. Not to be dismissed. Even as dimensions traverse each other, silence traverses the names it elides. Much as love's labyrinthine ear delights in the phrases it needs to hear, the unspoken truth grows clearer by day. There never was all that much to say. Old powers yield to new constraints. The demon of analogy is now a saint. We've had enough of plodders and schemers. Best to take up with makers and dreamers. They love their work, so save your praise for those who bring comfort to your latter days. It wasn't by chance we smashed the plates that proclaimed the Law of the Father. It's the only law we ever knew, but it isn't worth the bother.

12.

The resident Chimera loves these clouds. Euclid found them strange. Apart from its ruins, history is weightless. Rain carries molecules as old as Earth. Older by far than the first habitations, whose builders knew our thirst. Where locals resist any further austerities, thoughts arise of the old duality, from each according to each. Other tasks speak to other needs. It's time to summon our guardian angel and bring her up to speed. She it is who will guide us home, despite our premonitions. And that's the moment life jumps in with all its preconditions. Even as life holds a mirror to nature, the angel holds us back from the brink. Beyond which stretches the fecund Void. This is important, more than you think. Because that's where these songs were first deployed.

RETURN TO SILENCE

Piensa el sentimiento, siente el pensamiento.

— Miguel de Unamuno

1.

I write of necessity
    from a place apart.

        They say the fate of
            the nation is at hand.

    But then it always was.

I find no dignity in
    the suffering of

        others, but much
            in their struggle

    to survive.

And, as metaphors
    of struggle surmise,

        the fact remains
          we will not rise

    unless we rise together.

2.

From Aligheri's dark woods to
Baudelaire's forest of symbols;

from the voluptuary's garden
       of somber angels to the bridge
              that leads to the Underworld;

from your impudent beauty
       to your melancholy eyes, phantoms
              of active desire arise.

From here to immortality,
the future's a formality.

From one redacted draft
       to the next, the pages
              lost were legion.

"From one who has grown
       weary of life" is a poem by an
              ancient Egyptian.

Millennia later — and it still is news —
Langston called it The Weary Blues.

3.

The goddess traffics in infinite things and
sings at length of her shameless pleasures.

> There are some things that you can't
> make up. That's because they're real.

How will we know where we're headed
when we don't know where we've been?

> Note how objects transform themselves
> when their names belie their purposes.

What makes serious music serious?
Why not leave this canvas blank?

> Is it art when we tell tales
> of an evening dark and dank.

For countless ages, the empire of night
has pimped out the stars for our delight.

> Now that the goddess has left the stage,
> lay down your lessons. It's time to play.

4.

Electric eyes
minister

to passing
strangers.

Whose breath
is her song

has revived
our spirits.

Insolent spring
has long since

departed. Dust
devils rise

from drought-
stricken fields.

She, who
watches, waits.

5.

There must be a place from which this storied moment could be unriddled. The source of poetry's desire for itself is obscure if also compelling. It came in the form of a false memory. One that recalled an imaginary dream from a past that never happened. A curious scenario. One for the books. And yet the poem is true.

§

The dead have come to admonish us. We forget their travails at our peril. Every illusion of freedom we possess derives from their persistence — which is otherwise known as the story of culture, fragile as it may be. The sun will still burn for billions of years, which none will live to see.

§

To invent a language from within language is the very mark of the human. Where fiction proposes imaginary worlds, some more familiar than others, poetry proposes *this* world otherwise. In either case, there are provocations. Answers yet to be laid to rest. And questions yet to be raised.

§

The ascent to Parnassus is littered with failures. And each next one poses work to be done. The transformation from work to text reflects a mirror image. Your best intentions reside in the tain. When reading and writing came of age, they reinforced an ancient spell that has left you in thrall to the page.

6.

Poetry first became poetry when it took

up the musical phrase. Phonotactics set
the tune while contents shifted phase.

Wait for it, and something will happen.
Step by step, as befits our practice,
unchained melodies follow in kind.

While harmony dwells on the *y*-axis,
structure's a matter of working parts.
Therefore, syntax and the time it takes
to build the poem by fits and starts.

Why this obsession with cause and effect?
Given that everything's interdependent,
What did you think was yours to perfect?

You wouldn't notice the irregularities
if you weren't expecting a steady beat.

In quotable lines lie irrational feet.

7.

The last time Orpheus

    disobeyed, Eurydice paid

        with her life. Hence,

her loss gave birth to

    longing, which became his

        signature meme. Given

the limited number of

    themes whose import

        shapes our interpretive

schemes, what makes us hope

    for a different outcome,

        if only in our dreams?

8.

Our tradition is to break with tradition.
        Form must satisfy the limits it invents.

        Surrender is fundamental to the art. Given
that something is not nothing, nothing is

surely something else. Parallel lines may
        never meet and yet not be opposed. To say

        that poetry is self-directed is to say that
it shifts for itself. Even as we dwell in

a world of words, so do these words
        predicate a world that reminds us of all

        that we've lost. All, but not all. Desire
persists. As does our love of beauty.

For which we'd go to any length.
        Whose weakness is our strength.

9.

Not on your life,

                                       but life as such.

So how about

                                       those silences?

Language claims

                                       to make meaning.

Is form so difficult

                                       to grasp?

Odd little strophes,

                                       beginning to end.

Come back soon.

                                       Bring a friend.

10.

The Annals say
      all things return
            to their roots,

                  but this song
                        ends with a
                              flatted fifth.

My friend
      writes epigrams
            "on the rocks."

                  It appears we've
                        been found
                              wanting.

Not that there's
      any one thing
            they can point to.

                  And *that* was
                        the problem
                              all along.

11.

What history excludes is
        condemned to obscurity.
                Stillborn classics rule
                        the day. The poem exists
                                on its own terms. But,

be that as it may, who
        will exercise oversight?
                First, the elders. Then,
                        our comrades. And then
                                my "hypocrite lecteur."

This resembles the order of
        bloom. Especially when new
                tropes burst upon the scene
                        by reference, by rapport,
                                or by relation. Natural

languages follow a
        protocol. Syntax emerges,
                from which comes melody.
                        Then pulse, which ushers in
                                the silent music of things.

12.

The poet sprawled before the fire. His role was far from clear.
Meanwhile, locally sourced ontologies clung to the Middle Path.
Which is not to be mistaken for the Via Dolorosa. Much less the
Delta's fabled crossroads. Stoics prefer moderation to martyrdom.
Faint overtures of hope still reside within the future anterior. It's
there we will have pierced the veil of mastery. And what's the
good of that? It would appear our desires have been misinformed.
You try living on a dollar and a dream. In fact, why not try living
with yourself? Given your regrettable taste in men, Augustine
remains a viable source for putting some spin on your sin. And
your chimera says that even self-denial amounts to a passive form
of abuse. Hence, the poet in fragments, sundered by the crowd.
And no, my friend, we do not forgive. They knew what they were
doing. That's why the next time we build Babel, we'll exclude
the poetic function. Which seems extreme, but not to worry. The
gods will never notice nor the tourists ever know. Where writing
intersects the discourse on writing, there's little back and forth.
Parallel lives may never meet, but they know of the Grail we seek.
Now it's time to stoke the fire and bid the poet speak.

13.

It's hard going

        without a song.

    Breathe deep.

        Live long.

Music includes inaudible phenomena. Apropos of the light
fantastic, where sounds are movements determined by chance,
"See the music. Hear the dance."

     Pure disinterest

        shuns acclaim.

    A headstone waits on

        a date and a name.

Hard truths occupy local space-time. Unchained melodies break
the frame. Once we're working, our practice reveals, what affect
teaches, we think to feel.

14.

A finite being runs

    the gamut of love.

        Nothing stands in its way.

    Neither are life and death

        at odds when lovers

           part at break of day.

Our attention caught

    between being and not,

        we note subtle changes in

    the lighting. From cause to

        effect by skillful means.

           We see not what we saw.

15.

This concerto has been transcribed for double clarinets. The composer let imperfections in the score define random pitch events. The resulting run on the keyboard blended blues and consequence. Success is a fiction where failure rings true. There are etudes yet to be written when there's fuck-all else to do.

What are
the extremes
to which
we must go?

Who claims
to think
might claim
to know.

The point is to leave room for what comes next. Forget the author. Read the text. Not that it matters to you, nor should it. Not that it matters to the words we write. On a winter day, both cold and bright, what's caught on the wing remains our ideal. Thus, this billboard near Half Moon Bay: "Our cows are outstanding in their field."

16.

Time is the medium in which we

    dwell because of our attachment

to existence. Indeed, our silence

        knows only duration. Are you

      deaf to our pleas by design?

        There's plenty of nothing

to go around, but it doesn't

    take requests. Nor do public

accolades always sort the best.

       Hence, these voices from

     out of nowhere — where our

      ancestors take their rest.

17.

Invention embraces
things unseen.
And so it was that
the notion of an
impasse all but
stymied the builders.
Where differences
marked our
passage through
time and helped
us parse our days.

Not for nothing,
but something
got built. Some
thing more and
other than what
we first thought
of it. And from
which a form
resulted that
came to include
an impasse.

18.

Who slept hard by heaven in a fifth-floor walk-up, ciphered the
city's eclogues by night. The midst of life's journey had come
and gone. Mornings were given to coffee and contemplation.
"To praise the senses' raptures and the mind's." Then began the
daily grind, bellying up to the keyboard. Who wrote in order to
provoke a response but weighed each word with care. Weighed
them, in fact, until Happy Hour, when the scene from his aerie
was the end of an age. Whether we choose to admit it or not,
our presence has been a disaster. Now, as the ice caps melt away,
we're approaching a slough of despair. Where dominion was the
presiding virtue, reality *just is* the coming extinction. For which
(forgive us) we are not prepared.

19.

Throwing the dice was a moment of crisis disguised as an act of

will. Thus ended the Age of Classics in the decomposition

of the very elements that had made their readers who they were.

> *Your sacrifice persuades us that*
> *your fellowship has legs. Look*
> *how durable that meme on the*
> *cross has been since it first went*
> *viral. But how survive the*
> *coming extinction? And how*
> *survive each other? Only now do*
> *we think to ask, who have since*
> *run out of time.*

You knew you needed a change of scene when you asked for

water and they gave you gasoline. Hexameters call for six

the hard way. The blues rarely wants for reason or rhyme.

20.

The unsaid
          rests between
                    silences.

          An aporia
                    ably addresses
                              the twisted

                              logic of
                                        presence.

          A symptom
                    or cipher has
                              gone missing.

                    Duration is
                              essential to
                                        our lasting

                                        sense of
                                                  things.

21.

There was nothing untoward
about these conventions, but
of course we hoped for better.

          Serendipity left us songs aside.
          Torch and twang at midnight.
          A child's serenade at dawn.

That which he loathes
threatens all he loves. It is
a most singular compact.

          Awake to the world in
          its darkest hour, he rose
          to sing at break of day.

Childhood's end had
just begun. His lyrics
spoke to all but one.

          His repertoire rivaled
          the mockingbird, who
          also rose with the sun.

22.

Suppose we abandon these speech acts to their fate?
These eccentric fictions to their droll inconclusions?
These enigmas to the genres they inhabit?

> *Distinctive traits say what things are.*
> *But, we ask, being none the wiser,*
> *what makes them distinctive?*

Suppose we abandon these speech acts to their fate?
We must answer even at the cost of some disorder.
There are life skills at the crossroads for sale or lease.

> *You have paved your way with*
> *good intentions. Hence, your*
> *debt to the Devil as well.*

Suppose we abandon these speech acts to their fate —
and do so on behalf of our altogether other? That's as
close as we're going to get to the source of our desire.

> *Even as poetry commits to Nothing,*
> *Nothing commits to everything*
> *when "it is full of Being."*

23.

Who is this subject
        who would break
these bonds? Whose

                    desires are those
            of the one he desires.
                    Who bows deeply

to the Four Noble
        Truths, subject
to further analysis.

                    Intuition as a mode
            of knowing has not
                    been reckoned with.

Experience teaches
        the poem to navigate
between the rock

                    that we call silence
            and the hard place
                    we call language.

24.

Winter repossesses

       what little light remains
          to restore the present to

               its former splendor.

We've established

       a protocol for lost languages.
        The time of reckoning

              is now at hand.

Late in the season,
we assume the mantle

to the distant strains

of ghostly laughter.
There is work to be

done — and there

are songs to be
sung — before we

return to silence.

Ted Pearson was born and raised in Palo Alto, California. He began writing poetry in 1964 and subsequently attended Vandercook College of Music, Foothill College, and San Francisco State. His first book, *The Grit*, appeared in 1976. He has since published twenty-six books of poetry, including *Extant Glyphs: 1964 –1980* (2014), *An Intermittent Music: 1975 –2010* (2016) and his most recent, *Set Pieces* (2021). He also co-authored *The Grand Piano* (2006 – 2010), a ten-volume experiment in collective autobiography. He now lives in Houston, Texas.

Other books from selva oscura press

Why Letter Ellipsis by Kimberly Alidio

Alameda by Broc Rossell

Mood Indigo by Jeanne Heuving

Veronica: A Suite in X Parts by Erica Hunt

Eroding Witness by Nathaniel Mackey

afterKleist by Matthew Fink

A Spell in the Pokey: Selected Poems by Hugh Walthall edited by Aldon Lynn Nielsen

Zippers & Jeans by J. Peter Moore

Moment's Omen by Nathaniel Mackey

dog with elizabethan collar by Ken Taylor

And by Three Count Pour
(an imprint of selva oscura press)

Breath and Precarity by Nathaniel Mackey

No Hierarchy of the Lovely: Ten Uncollected Essays and Other Prose 1939–1981 by Robert Duncan
edited by James Maynard

Songs In-Between the Day / Offshore St. Mark by David Need
—Durham Suite: 5—

Anuncio's Last Love Song by Nathaniel Mackey

Southern Colortype by J. Peter Moore

first the trees, now this by Ken Taylor

A History of Fire by Dianne Timbin

[Distressed Properties] by Magdalena Zurawski

selvaoscurapress.com